Getting Over The Blues:

A Kid's Guide to Understanding and Coping with Unpleasant Feelings and Depression

by

Kim "Tip" Frank, Ed.S., LPC
Counselor/Psychotherapist
Rock Hill School District
Family Counseling and
    Play Therapy Services
Rock Hill, SC

Susan J. Smith-Rex, Ed.D.
Professor of Special Education
College of Education
Winthrop University
Rock Hill, SC

Illustrations coordinated by Ruth Ann Jackson
Cover drawing by John Wilson

Copyright 1996

Educational Media Corporation®
P.O. Box 21311
Minneapolis, MN 55421-0311

(763) 781-0088 or (800) 966-3382

http://www.**educationalmedia**.com

ISBN 0-932796-75-3

Library of Congress Catalog No. 96-83775

Printing (Last Digit)

9 8 7 6 5 4 3

Production editor-

Don L. Sorenson, Ph.D.

Graphic Design-

Earl Sorenson

Illustrations-

The following students at Northwestern High School in Rock Hill, South Carolina: **Jamie Busby, Casey Cook, Maggie McCaskill, Eve Najim, Emily Nunnery, Curt Mattes, Ann Price, Kari Ramsey, Mary Salamonski, Corrie Sexton, Erick Smith, Justin Smith, Frank Vickery, Mike Weeks, Rick Williams, and John Wilson**

Special thanks to Dawn Head of Fort Mill, South Carolina, who has helped in the writing of this book by trying and succeeding at many of the ideas.

Kim "Tip" Frank, Ed.S., LPC and Susan J. Smith-Rex, Ed.D.

Note to parents and health professionals:

This book is intended to aid children in dealing with their feelings. The book was carefully written to be user friendly for children. We trust the vocabulary, illustrations, and limited number of words on each page will make this book inviting and helpful to children in their understanding of unpleasant feelings and depression.

The second part of this book focuses on practical ideas children can use to better cope with their feelings. We believe in children's abilities to work out problems in their own lives. This section is interactive in nature. The student selects areas of concern and does activities which will help the child to explore what needs to be done to best cope. In essence, mental health projects are provided that are practical and thought provoking.

While the book can be used independently by elementary and middle school students, we highly recommend parents and mental health professionals read and discuss this book with children. In this way the information and suggestions are fully discussed and the children are encouraged to follow through on the coping strategies provided. Best wishes as you put this book to good use!

Kim "Tip" Frank, Ed.S., LPC

Susan J. Smith-Rex, Ed.D.

Table of Contents

Part I
Helping Children Understand and Cope with Unhappy Feelings and Depression

Jamie Busby

When a child is born, he or she is given certain physical and mental characteristics that for the most part are there throughout his or her life.

Kim "Tip" Frank, Ed.S., LPC and Susan J. Smith-Rex, Ed.D.

Maggie McCaskill

Children vary in many ways, such as the size of their bodies, color of skin, texture of hair, shape of their noses, color and strength of their eyes, learning ability of their brains, and the health of their body organs.

Eve Najim

Whether people are satisfied with the way they look or how they feel will vary according to their ages, the reactions they get from other people, and the choices that are available to them.

Maggie McCaskill

Everyone likes to feel they have some control over the way their lives are going. The truth is you may have more control than you realize.

Mike Weeks

Self-esteem is an important characteristic that develops inside persons over time as a result of the ways they feel their lives are being shaped.

Maggie McCaskill

It is important to work at developing a positive self-esteem because with it comes many good feelings and pleasurable emotions.

Corrie Sexton

Emotions are intense feelings that range from love and happiness all the way to anger, disappointment, and even hopelessness.

Kim "Tip" Frank, Ed.S., LPC and Susan J. Smith-Rex, Ed.D.

Curt Mattes

Emotions are felt by all people every day. Emotions are a normal part of life. How we react to our feelings can either be helpful or hurtful. To a large extent this choice can only be controlled by you.

Eric Smith

Although everyone will feel positive or pleasant feelings as well as negative or unpleasant feelings during life, it is important to not get "stuck" on unpleasant feelings for long periods of time.

Kim "Tip" Frank, Ed.S., LPC and Susan J. Smith-Rex, Ed.D.

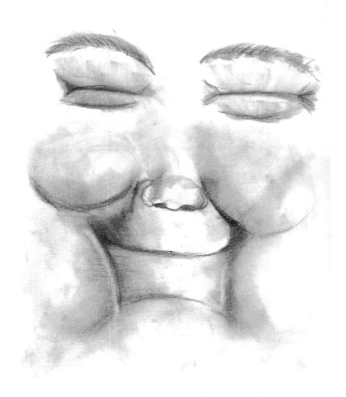

Positive thinking is so important to our good health and happiness. It allows us to set goals and gives us hope that our efforts will pay off.

Eve Najim

Negative thinking is a destructive waste of energy. It can lead to a problem called depression.

Curt Mattes

Depression is a disorder from which many children suffer today. Roughly one out of every seven Americans will suffer from extended depression sometime during their life. It is a disorder of which young people need to be aware. How does it happen, how does it create other problems, and how can you prevent it from happening to you? These are questions we will help you consider.

Mike Weeks

Kim "Tip" Frank, Ed.S., LPC and Susan I. Smith-Rex, Ed.D.

Mike Weeks

Depression in children often begins by not feeling well received by others. Other times a stressful event happens such as parents divorcing, the death of a loved one, problems at school or home, and so forth. This can trigger negative thinking and feelings. If one doesn't consciously turn those negative thoughts in a positive direction, then physical and emotional problems are likely to occur.

Negative thinking can cause a person to feel some of these ways:

- *Your stomach or throat feels tied up like a knot.*
- *You can't sleep well or you sleep too much.*
- *You lose or gain too much weight.*
- *You can't concentrate in school.*
- *You seem to have little interest in most activities.*
- *You have low energy levels.*
- *You think about hurting others.*
- *You feel worthless or guilty.*
- *You have suicidal thoughts.*
- *You retreat into your own world, not wanting to be around others.*
- *You say things and do things you don't really mean.*
- *You have more headaches than normal.*

Anne Price

Depressed children often find it difficult to set goals because they believe they will fail. School and social problems are more likely when no effort or motivation is present.

Maggie McCaskill

Depressed students often abandon peers who are thinking positive thoughts in favor of new peers who are also doing poorly. This can lead to a very destructive pattern of behavior.

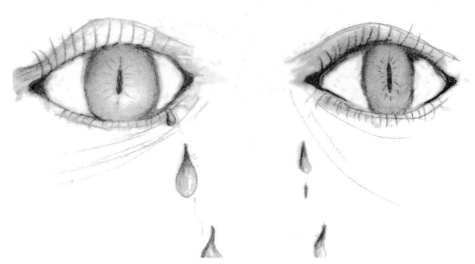

Eve Najim

Depression can range from very mild to severe. Mild depression is common when a sad or unfortunate event takes place, such as a death in the family, an illness, or a change in one's life. Mild depression ordinarily lasts for a short period of time, and the person understands that the event is causing the sad feelings.

John Wilson

More serious or long lasting depression seems to happen over and over again. Oftentimes there seems to be no apparent reason for the intense feelings of sadness. This type of depression creeps up on a person. The person thinks, "I can snap out of it." However, serious depression is not easily shaken.

Mary Salamonski

The person with depression may feel guilty and blame him or herself for not breaking out of the slump. If you are depressed, please know it is not your fault. No one wants or chooses to be depressed. The fact of the matter is that long lasting depression is a physical disease. It is a physical problem as much as cancer or diabetes is. In the same way a diabetic lacks enough insulin to process sugar, some people lack sufficient chemicals to permit their brain to function properly. This is called a chemical imbalance.

Rick Williams

When depression becomes serious, persons may feel powerless to solve their problems and may turn to drugs, alcohol, or even suicidal thoughts to try and make the hopelessness disappear.

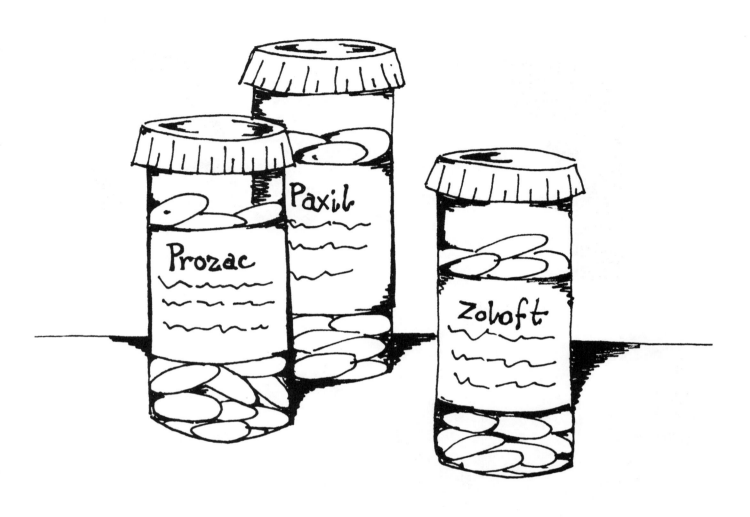

Maggie McCaskill

Some people who are depressed can be helped by medication called antidepressants. Antidepressants help balance chemicals in your brain. Simply said, certain medications make the brain work correctly. If medication is needed to cope with depression, it sometimes takes your doctor time to get the right medication for you. There are several antidepressants such as Prozac®, Paxil®, Wellbutrin® and Zoloft® among others. This may mean some trial and error in finding the right amount and type of medication. This is done under the careful supervision of a doctor.

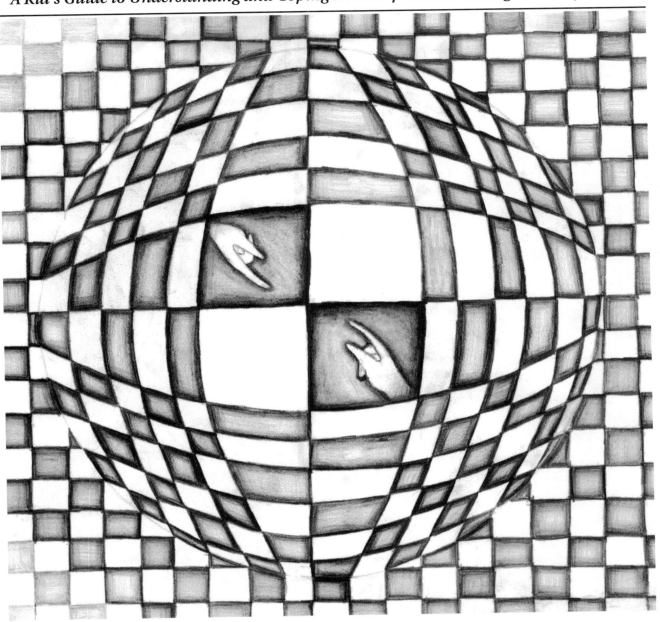

Frank Vickery

In most cases, overcoming long lasting depression takes several weeks or perhaps months. Most people experience gradual improvement with counseling and the help of a doctor. The lifting of depression is like fog burning off in the morning sun. Some people even experience depression more than once. Thankfully it can be treated as before and you can go on again with your life. Don't give up! It can and will get better!

Justin Smith

One thing to understand about depression is that it often runs in families. Chances are good that if you are dealing with depression, someone related to you really understands what you are experiencing. Sometimes these people can really help since they have been there.

Kim "Tip" Frank, Ed.S., LPC and Susan J. Smith-Rex, Ed.D.

John Wilson

People with depression often get into a pattern of thinking negatively or in ways that make things worse.

John Wilson

What are some of the common thinking errors of depressed students?

1. *Magnifying—Things or problems look bigger than they really are.*

2. *Jumping to Conclusions—Thinking the worst will happen.*

3. *All or Nothing Thinking—Things are great or terrible.*

4. *Taking Things Personally—When you take responsibility for things that happened which may have been out of your control.*

One of the first steps to "getting over the blues" is to take control of any negative thinking that is going on inside you. You need to replace negative thoughts with good thoughts that can help you to work out problems and feel better about yourself. Later in our book, this is discussed in greater detail. Read on!

Maggie McCaskill

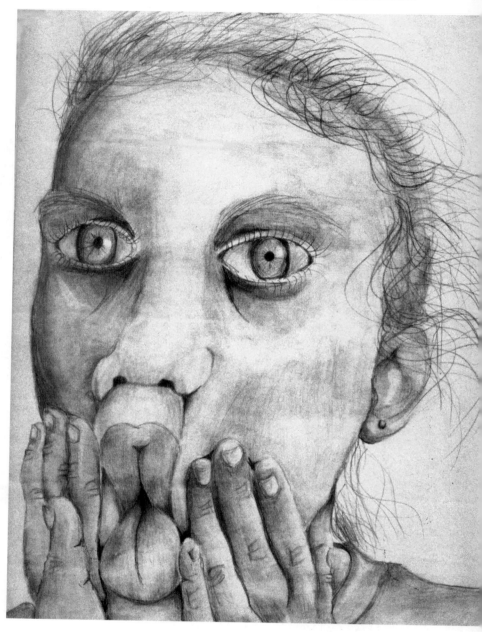

Eve Najim

Why do some children just have a way about them that tells others they are basically happy, fun kids? What are some of their mannerisms that make them more likable? Do they:

- *Smile a lot?*
- *Not wish bad things for others?*
- *Use positive self-statements?*
- *Not act jealous of those who are doing well?*
- *Say nice things about other people?*
- *Do what is expected of them on time and without complaining?*
- *Talk to people first and ask how they are?*
- *Have a support team that they talk to often?*
- *Reach out to help someone else?*
- *Realize that some things are out of their control?*

Kim "Tip" Frank, Ed.S., LPC and Susan J. Smith-Rex, Ed.D.

Emily Nunnery

These positive qualities, that anyone can do, will help you also to be well received by family, friends, and classmates. Being well received creates positive thinking so you can more adequately deal with life's ups and downs that everybody has.

Mike Weeks

People perceive life's events very differently. For example, moving to a new town may be seen either as a loss or an adventure. Thus, it is not necessarily the event but the views we take of the event that please or upset us.

Casey Cook

Some people think feelings come from the things that happen to us, but oftentimes it is our perception or the way a person looks at things that makes the real difference.

Jamie Busby

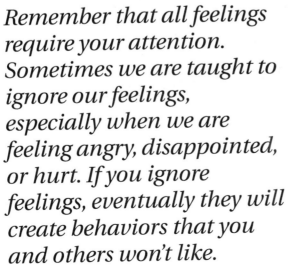

It is important to pay attention to your thoughts each day. If left unaddressed, negative thinking can become a bad habit.

Kari Ramsey

Remember that all feelings require your attention. Sometimes we are taught to ignore our feelings, especially when we are feeling angry, disappointed, or hurt. If you ignore feelings, eventually they will create behaviors that you and others won't like.

Educational Media Corporation®, Box 21311, Minneapolis, MN 55421-0311

Jamie Busby

Everybody needs someone who will listen and understand. People with whom you feel comfortable can help you to express your feelings and set reasonable goals so you can "get over the blues" and get on with your life.

Kim "Tip" Frank, Ed.S., LPC and Susan J. Smith-Rex, Ed.D.

Part II

Practical Ideas to Cope with Unpleasant Feelings and Depression

In order to better deal with depression, we have identified five good things you can do to help yourself. Think about which ones you may need to consider and turn to the pages that are shown for some helpful ideas.

Take good care of yourself. You're worth it.

Mental Health Projects

1. **Learning the Facts About Depression:**
   What is depression and how does it affect me?
   (Turn to page 39.)

2. **Detecting Automatic Negative Thinking:**
   Changing muddy messages to clear messages.
   (Turn to page 43.)

3. **Evaluating Thoughts and Feelings:**
   Recognizing — Relaxing —Feeling Better
   (Turn to page 49.)

4. **Anger Management:**
   Handling anger in a positive way.
   (Turn to page 58.)

5. **Taking Control of My Life:**
   Making good choices to make my life better.
   (Turn to page 60.)

Kim "Tip" Frank, Ed.S., LPC and Susan J. Smith-Rex, Ed.D.

Terms

Addiction - When a person depends upon a drug to deal with life.

Anger management - To handle anger in a positive way to help anger go away without hurting anyone.

Anxiety - A feeling of fearful uneasiness or worry about what may happen.

At Risk - People more likely to suffer problems of depression because of either having someone in their family who struggles with depression or social problems in their lives.

Clear messages - When a person thinks good thoughts about himself or herself.

Coping skills - Positive ways to act so you can feel good about yourself and begin solving any problems.

Defenses - Walls we create to hide true feelings: joking, daydreaming, talking back, silence, blaming, constant talking, using drugs.

Depression - The emotion of feeling sad, blue, and unhappy.

Emotions - Intense feelings that range from love and happiness to anger, disappointment, and hopelessness.

Muddy messages - When a person thinks bad thoughts about himself or herself.

Perceptions - The way a person views or thinks about something.

Poor self-esteem - When a person feels of little or no worth.

Reality checking - When you ask yourself what proof there is to believe what you are thinking.

Reframing thoughts - When you learn to look at a situation in the best way possible.

Strategy - A careful plan for achieving a goal.

Support System - Community helpers and family to whom you can turn for help.

Are You Depressed?

Circle yes or no to the following questions. Do you:

1. Eat too much or too little?	Yes	No
2. Have trouble sleeping too much or too little?	Yes	No
3. Feel restless or slowed down?	Yes	No
4. Have a loss of interest or pleasure in doing usual activities?	Yes	No
5. Feel worthless and think bad thoughts about yourself?	Yes	No
6. Have difficulty concentrating?	Yes	No
7. Often think about death or suicide?	Yes	No
8. Often feel irritated or in a bad mood?	Yes	No
9. Feel fatigue or loss of energy nearly everyday?	Yes	No

If you answered yes to several of these, you may be depressed. A good rule of thumb is to talk to your counselor or doctor if you have had these symptoms for more than a few days.

1. Learning the Facts About Depression: What is depression and how does it affect me?

Mark True or False for each statement.

T   F

❏   ❏   1. Depression is a disease that tends to affect everyone in the family in some way.

❏   ❏   2. About one in seven people during their lives will suffer from extended depression.

❏   ❏   3. Depression occurs more frequently with girls than boys.

❏   ❏   4. Students struggling with depression are more likely to miss school, have poor grades, have fewer friends, and consider activities that are not in their best interest.

❏   ❏   5. Treatment for student depression is a problem because of denial and a lack of referrals to counselors.

❏   ❏   6. Heredity plays a part in many cases of depression.

❏   ❏   7. Most children who struggle with depression do so because of negative thinking about themselves and their lives.

❏   ❏   8. High levels of stress can trigger depression.

❏   ❏   9. Depression can be overcome through counseling and in many cases through the use of medication.

❏   ❏   10. Depression may result from the brain being low in certain chemical substances which causes the brain not to function properly.

see page 64 for the answers

Charting My Feelings

It is important to pay attention to your feelings each day. One good way to do this is to keep a Day Chart for your feelings. Using a Day Chart helps you to see patterns in your emotions. You will be able to note events or situations that bring about pleasant or unpleasant feelings. You will also be more aware of slumps. Slumps are periods of several days when you are having unpleasant feelings. In such cases, we recommend that you talk to people you trust to help turn your feelings around. A good rule of thumb is that after two days of unpleasant feelings, you should seek out someone in your support system with whom you can discuss your situation and feelings.

The following is a made-up example of a Day Chart. Notice the scale of 1 to 10 to rate your feelings, which is done three times daily. Also, an average score is figured for the three parts of the day. (Just add up your three scores for morning, afternoon, and evening and then divide by three. Don't worry about remainders.)

Make several copies of the blank Day Chart on page 41 and keep track of how your days are going. As we mentioned earlier, if you see a pattern of low scores, talk it over with someone you trust. As you learn ways to cope and work out problems, your score is bound to rise.

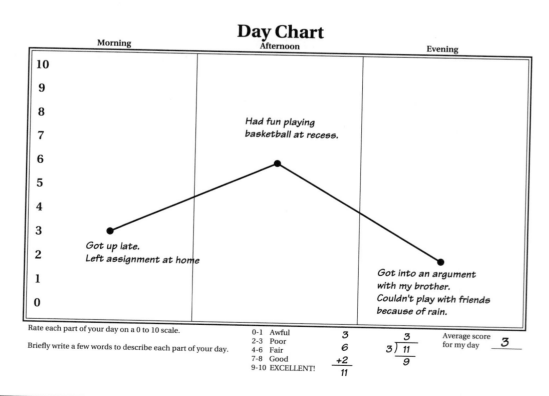

Day Chart

Rate each part of your day on a 0 to 10 scale.

Briefly write a few words to describe each part of your day.

0-1	Awful
2-3	Poor
4-6	Fair
7-8	Good
9-10	EXCELLENT!

Kim "Tip" Frank, Ed.S., LPC and Susan J. Smith-Rex, Ed.D.

Day Chart

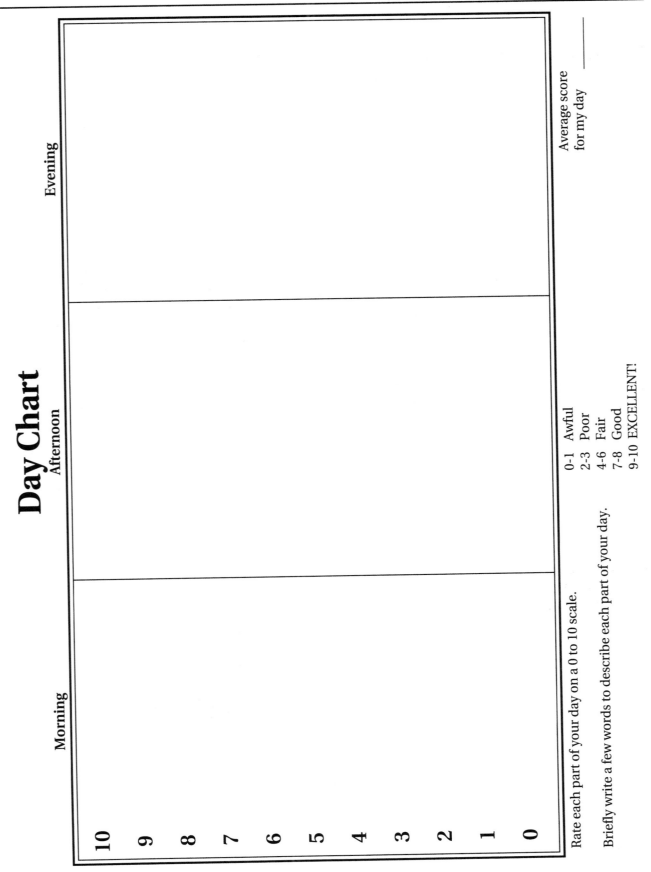

Morning	Afternoon	Evening
10		
9		
8		
7		
6		
5		
4		
3		
2		
1		
0		

Rate each part of your day on a 0 to 10 scale.

Briefly write a few words to describe each part of your day.

0-1	Awful
2-3	Poor
4-6	Fair
7-8	Good
9-10	EXCELLENT!

Average score for my day _____

Identifying Support at School

In your school, there is likely a support group for children dealing with various problems. Ask your counselor or a teacher for information about small group counseling. Support groups help you to see that you are not the only one dealing with the problems. Many kids your age meet to encourage each other and to discuss ideas for coping. The group offers a safe place for you to discuss your feelings and to enjoy being with others.

Helpful People

Just as important as an ongoing support group are individuals with whom you feel comfortable discussing your situation. Your school counselor and other trusted adults can be counted on to be helpful. It is a good idea to build a network of caring people, both adults and children. Trusted adults may include a parent, coach, teacher, counselor, best friend's mother, religious leader, and so forth.

Friendships with peers may grow out of a support group and other activities in which you may participate. Clubs and after school activities are a good way to develop friendships and to focus on good things that will help you to move along with life.

What does your support team look like? Fill in as many circles as possible. Be sure to include individuals and groups who are helpful to you. Remember, you don't have to be the "Lone Ranger." There are many people who care. You can develop your support team as large as you would like. It seems to gradually grow as you reach out.

**Individuals and Groups
That Make Up
My Support Team**

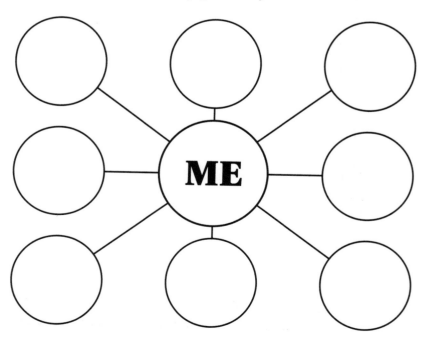

Kim "Tip" Frank, Ed.S., LPC and Susan J. Smith-Rex, Ed.D.

2. Detecting Automatic Negative Thinking

People so often have thoughts that cause problems for them. Thoughts like, "It's terrible; I can't stand it; everything is awful;" etc. get us into trouble. These types of thoughts bring about unhappy feelings and cause our behavior to be less than our best. If left unnoticed, these unhelpful thoughts become a bad habit. We call them **ANT**, which stands for **A**utomatic **N**egative **T**hinking.

Automatic   —   being unaware or not noticing

Negative   —   bad

Thinking   —   what you believe about a situation

So, Automatic Negative Thinking means having bad or unhelpful thoughts that just happen over and over.

Like ants, they can cover you in no time and cause you to be miserable. Instead of being miserable, we want you to become **ANT** killers. **ANT** killing involves catching and killing your negative thoughts as you notice them. In this way, you don't allow yourself to think in negative, unhelpful ways. You instead learn to replace them with good thoughts that help you to work out problems and feel better about yourself. See mental health project on page 49 called the Three R's which talks about changing your way of thinking in positive ways.

The following is a list of thoughts from the ANT hill. Try to catch these thoughts before they cause you problems. Circle any automatic negative thoughts which you have that need to be killed.

ANT Hill

1. It's just **awful**.

2. I **can't stand it**.

3. It **makes me** mad.

4. I'll just **die** if it doesn't go my way.

5. I **can't handle** it.

6. I'll be happy **when things change**.

7. **If only** things were different, I'd feel better.

8. This is the **worst** thing.

9. I **must** have this.

10. It **just figures** this would happen.

11. He **shouldn't** act that way.

12. Life is **always** bad.

13. **Everything** is just awful.

14. What a **bummer**!

15. That **stinks**!

16. This could **only** happen to me.

Notice the circled words. Become aware of these words that most of us tend to use too often and become an ANT killer.

Clear Messages

I'm thinking of a person who is very important and special. This person is someone you see every day. This person is also one of the most important friends you could ever have. Can you name this person?

The answer is *YOU!* Sometimes we forget to be thankful for the good things in our lives when we are confused with family problems. One thing to keep in mind is that very few families are perfect. Feeling sad all the time is unproductive and will hurt your self-esteem.

The best way to feel better about yourself is to change your way of thinking. Your thinking gets you into trouble. It can also get you out of trouble. You have basically two ways of thinking about yourself and the things that happen to you. We call them muddy messages and clear messages.

Muddy messages are thoughts that cause you to feel bad about yourself. You feel upset inside and things bother you.

Clear messages are just the opposite. Your thoughts make you feel good about yourself. You feel at peace inside and things don't bother you.

Here are some examples of clear versus muddy thinking.

Event	Muddy Message	Clear Message
Someone calls you a name.	"Everyone thinks I'm a jerk."	"People who call names are just trying to get others upset. I'm not going to pay attention to him."
You failed a test.	"What's the point in trying? I'll never pass this class. I'm dumb in math."	"I wish I would have done better. However, I'm still an O.K. person. I'll get some help and do better next time."

This is called *self-talk.* What you say to yourself makes all the difference. To feel good about yourself, it is important to think good thoughts. Good thoughts equal good feelings. Remember we all have things we're not really good at doing. It is okay not to be good at some things. What's important is to do your best and learn to like yourself.

One of the most important self-talk words to remember is *IALAC.* It stands for I Am Lovable and Capable. *Lovable* means people can love you just because of who you are. You are special not because of what you do but who you are. *Capable* means you can. You can do many things well. Take a minute to list at least two things you do well at school and outside of school.

In School	**Out of School**
1. _____	1. _____
2. _____	2. _____

On an index card, write the word IALAC. Let this be your secret code word. Take it with you to remind you that you are special and O.K.

IALAC is a wonderful clear message. There are many more that you can say to yourself. Try the following experiment this week. Every time something happens to you good or bad, give yourself a clear message. Catch your muddy messages and change them to clear messages. Remember, you control what you think. No junk thoughts! Practice using clear messages such as:

"I'm O.K."

"I can handle it."

"I'll just do my best."

"No one is perfect."

"It's going to work out."

List some more clear messages you might give yourself.

1. _____

2. _____

3. _____

4. _____

How can you change automatic negative thoughts?

1. Chart your feelings.
2. Give positive self statements.
3. Realize that some things are out of your control.
4. Cognitive rehearsal - help to imagine yourself thinking differently than in the past.
5. Antiprocrastination - don't put off what needs to be done.
6. Reach out to others in a positive way.
7. Keep a diary.

Thinking - Feeling - Acting

Some people think feelings come from the things that happen to us.

For example, if your day begins by missing the morning alarm clock, you may feel panicked or upset because of being late or being behind schedule.

While being late or being behind schedule is not a good experience, it is easy to overreact.

This is not because of the situation. Rather, it is one's perception or the way a person looks at things that makes the difference.

Look at the following illustration of the train.

Think of your mind, emotions, and behavior as being like a small train. Notice your mind is the engine that drives the train. Your emotions and behavior follow behind.

In our example, does missing the alarm clock cause panic? Actually the answer is **NO**. Study the picture to see why?

Maggie McCaskill

Did you notice the "muddy message" he was giving himself, "I'll get killed if I'm late for school." It's not the lateness. It's his view of being late. It's key to stop and notice your thoughts about each situation. What else could he have said to himself? See the following picture.

Jamie Busby

Again, what happens to us is not as important as how we view each event or situation. A good way to understand this is by knowing your **ABC**'s.

I'm late, but it's not the end of the world.

A
Action or event
(Something that
happens to you)

B
Belief or Thought
(The message you
send to yourself)

C
Consequences or
what happens
(Feelings and Behaviors)

You cannot always control the things that happen to you such as being teased or having a friend move away. You can, however, control your thinking. Your thinking can be a "muddy message" or a "clear message."

Notice the difference in the outcome when "muddy" versus "clear messages" are used.

A
Missing the morning
alarm clock.
Being late for school.

B
(Muddy Message)
"I'll get killed if I'm
late for school."

C
Panic—upset feeling
Racing to get ready for
school.

or

A
Missing the morning
alarm clock.
Being late for school.

B
(Clear Message)
"I'm late, but it's not
the end of the world."

C
Hurried, but in control.
Gets to school in a
good state of mind.

Remember the letter **C** does not come after the letter **A**. **C** always follows **B**. Your Beliefs make all the difference. Work on keeping your messages to yourself clear.

3. Evaluating Thoughts and Feelings

A. The Three R's:
Recognizing, Reality Checking and Reframing

As mentioned earlier in our book, how we think about ourselves and the things that happen to us are key. Our perceptions (how we're looking at things) is often more important than the event that has happened to a person. While a person may not be able to control a lot of things that happen such as parents' divorce, moving, teasing, and so forth, we can always control our thinking. Our thoughts are very powerful and often make the difference between coping (handling the situation in a good way) or not coping (not handling the situation well).

Recognizing Thoughts

Clear thinking involves giving yourself permission to stop and think. This involves recognizing your thoughts and feelings.

Stop and ask yourself a couple of questions.

1. Why am I feeling the way I am?

2. What exactly are my thoughts about this situation?

For example, suppose my team lost an important game. I might ask myself, *"Why am I feeling so down in the dumps?"* Answer: I hated losing the game. What exactly are my thoughts about losing? Answer: *"It's awful we didn't win. It's the worst thing that could happen to us."*

Reality Checking

Next, do some reality checking. Ask yourself the following question to see if you are looking at the situation as it **really is**.

What proof (evidence) is there to believe this?

In the case above, what proof is there that it is awful and the worst thing that our team didn't win?

If I carefully examine my thoughts, I will realize that while losing is very disappointing, it is not the end of the world. No truly awful thing happened and I'll live to play another game.

Reframing Thoughts

Now that I've caught some of my negative thoughts, I can try reframing. Reframing involves looking at the situation in the best way possible. This is called positive thinking. Ask yourself one more question to start to get yourself thinking positively.

What is the best way to think about this situation?

In the case of losing the important game, I can see some things if I really look.

Yes, it is disappointing. We didn't win the game, but I can think about learning from this game and looking ahead to the next game. I can also feel good about giving it my best effort.

To summarize the three R's of thinking, look at the following examples.

Event

Our team lost an important game.

1. Recognizing My Thinking
(What are my thoughts?)

"It's awful. It's the worst thing that could happen."

2. Reality Checking
(What proof is there to believe this?)
"No, it's not the most awful or worst thing."

3. Reframing
My Thinking
(What is the best way to think about this?) "It's certainly disappointing, but we can learn from this and hopefully do better next time. We're still a good team."

The result is that I would feel disappointed but still good about myself. I would also learn something and look forward to the next game.

Now try your hand at the following examples of situations in which kids may find themselves. Use the three **R**'s to work through them.

Events:

Divorce of parents

Moving to another town

Some kids are teasing me

Recognizing My Thinking (What are my thoughts?)

Reality Checking (What proof is there to believe this?)

Reframing My Thinking (What is the best way to think about this?)

B. RASing Your Feelings

When it comes to feelings, you have all kinds. It is important to know how to handle feelings. The word **RAS** is another secret code word worth remembering. It can remind you of three important things to do with your feelings.

R stands for **R**ecognize Your Feelings.

Recognize means to know or to think about your feelings. You have two types of feelings. Here are some examples under each type.

Pleasant Feelings

(Feelings we like to have)

A. happy
B. excited
C. surprised
D. loved
E. confident
F. hopeful

Unpleasant Feelings

(Feelings we don't like to have)

G. sad
H. mad
I. frustrated
J. disappointed
K. scared
L. guilty
M. embarrassed
N. worried

Recognizing or knowing what feelings you have is very important. Throughout each day, stop for a minute and listen to your feelings. Ask, how am I feeling right now? Your body and mind will tell you.

For one entire week, using the chart on the next page, take a minute in the morning, after school, and before bed to identify your strongest feeling. Pick a feeling word from the list of pleasant and unpleasant feelings and put the letter in the appropriate box. At the end of the week add up how often each letter or feeling occurred.

A stands for **A**ccept Your Feelings.

Accept means that your feelings are always O.K. Accept means to take your feelings as they are. There is nothing wrong with feeling the way you do. Feelings are a part of you, and they are O.K.

S stands for **S**hare Your Feelings

Feelings are to be **shared** with others. Talking to people you trust about your feelings is a wonderful way to express your feelings. Feelings are not to be kept inside. You just feel better when you talk to others about your feelings. With whom can you share your feelings? Try to list at least three people whom you believe can be trusted with your deepest feelings.

Chart My Feelings

Time	Monday	Tuesday	Wednesday	Thursday	Friday	Saturday	Sunday
Morning							
Afternoon							
Evening							

- Write the letter for your strongest feeling three times a day for one week.
- Add up how often each feeling occurred
- Read section 5 of this book

Pleasant Feelings

(Feelings we like to have)

   A. happy

   B. excited

   C. surprised

   D. loved

   E. confident

   F. hopeful

Unpleasant Feelings

(Feelings we don't like to have)

   G. sad

   H. mad

   I. frustrated

   J. disappointed

   K. scared

   L. guilty

   M. embarrassed

   N. worried

C. Magic Button: Relaxing and Feeling Better

Your five senses of smelling, tasting, seeing, hearing, and touching work closely with your mind. Not only do your senses send important messages to your brain, they help create feelings. These feelings happen largely as a result of past experiences. For example, when you see a dog, your mind will recall past experiences involving dogs. These experiences may have been good, such as remembering times of playing with your favorite pet, or bad, such as being chased or bitten by a dog. Therefore, your feelings may be pleasant (happy, warm, etc.) or unpleasant (frightened, worried, etc.) depending on your experiences. Your mind has an amazing ability to bring back feelings of the past when situations occur. Think about the following situations and notice what feelings happen with yourself.

Event	My Feelings
1. Listening to the waves at the beach	
2. Hearing a bee fly nearby	
3. Smelling a flower	
4. Eating watermelon	
5. Getting a back rub	

Notice how certain feelings, some of them strong emotions, occurred. As stated earlier, the brain brings back feelings from the past. We can use this connection between your mind and senses to our advantage in order to relax and to improve our feelings. We call this "magic button." While it's really *not* magical, it seems like it is because depressed, anxious, and unhappy feelings can be washed away and replaced with happy and calm feelings.

Think of your brain as a computer that can be programmed by your sense of touch and by using your imagination. You pair or put together a mental image or picture in your mind with the sense of touch. There are a few steps in order to make this thing we call "magic button" work. First, list the types of feelings you would like to have. For example, happy, calm, confident, etc. (See page 53 for a list of feelings.)

1.

2.

3.

4.

5.

Next, focus on using your imagination. Think of good experiences of the past or imagine experiences you would like to have. Center your imagination around experiences that help create or make the feelings you would like to have. Using the list of feelings you would like to have, choose one feeling or possibly two feelings that are similar.

For example:

1. proud
2. excited
3. relaxed
4. happy
5. peaceful

Now, think of five to ten good experiences that help bring about the exact feelings you want.

For example:

Specific feeling(s) chosen	**Good experiences**
relaxed	1. Fishing in Canada
peaceful	2. Hiking in the mountains
	3. Riding my bike on the bike path
	4. Eating pizza with friends
	5. Watching a favorite TV show
	6. Playing catch with a baseball
	7. Calling a friend on the phone

Now, choose your own specific feeling(s) and list your good experiences.

My specific feeling(s)	**My good experiences**
that I would like to have	(list at least five)
_____	1. _____
_____	2. _____
_____	3. _____
_____	4. _____
_____	5. _____
_____	6. _____
_____	7. _____
_____	8. _____
_____	9. _____
_____	10. _____

At this point, we will "pair" or put together your sense of touch with the good experiences you've listed. As mentioned earlier, we call this "magic button." You will now need to choose a "magic button." Your magic button is simply a touch. It can be a touch on your elbow, knee, hip, etc. It can be a wiggle of a toe or finger. You decide for yourself. The only rule is that you do the exact touch each time for the same length of time. For example, you might wiggle your big toe three times or touch your elbow for three seconds. Again, the important thing to keep in mind is using your "magic button" the same way each time. Also, choose a magic button that is not very noticeable to others.

At this time, think of your "magic button" and write it down below.

My magic button: _____

Now, you are ready to "pair" your "magic button" with your good experiences that you listed before. To do this, simply picture your good experiences. When you experience the pleasant feelings you desire, push your magic button. Continue visualizing or picturing these good experiences over and over. When your desired feelings grow strong, push your magic button. As you practice this on a regular basis, more and more pleasant feelings are experienced. Once the connection between your magic button and feelings is made, you may use your magic button to bring about the feelings you want in seconds.

Suppose you've been practicing the use of your magic button for several days while picturing in your mind good experiences. When faced with unhappy feelings, you can push your magic button and replace feelings with the ones you want. This usually occurs within seconds. The key is to practice, practice, practice, so your magic button can turn your feelings around automatically. Also, note that you can have different magic buttons for different feelings which you desire to have. You use the same steps that we'll summarize at the end of this section. Some examples of magic buttons and specific feelings follow.

Specific Feelings	**Magic Button**
Happy	Touch knee
Confident (Good feelings about myself)	Wiggle toe two times
Excited (Full of energy)	Hold wrist

These, of course, are just examples. Many people have two or three magic buttons. Begin with one for starters. Once your first magic button is working well, you may want to work on another. Good luck as you try the steps of magic button which we will summarize. Many have found this to be a powerful way of overcoming unhappy feelings.

Summary of Magic Button Steps

1. Think of a specific feeling you want to have.
2. Make a list of good experiences you've had or would like to have that would help bring about the feeling you want.
3. Choose a magic button. Make sure your magic button touch or movement is the same each time.
4. Picture in your mind the good experiences you've listed. When your pleasant feeling is strong, push your magic button.
5. Practice step four regularly. The magic button connection to your desired feelings will become automatic.
6. Use your magic button during periods of time when you are having unpleasant feelings. This will wash them away and replace them with the pleasant feeling you want.

4. Anger Management: Handling Anger in a Positive Way

Probably the strongest of all emotions is anger, which is a critical factor to consider in the treatment of depression. While the feeling of anger is normal and OK to have, what one does with anger is crucial. A depressed individual feels guilty about not being able to express angry feelings directly at the object, person, or situation causing the frustration. Mishandling anger causes hurt and problems to the person and others. Handling anger in a positive way helps the anger to go away without harming anyone. There are three basic ways that people handle anger. See the following information and decide which way you usually deal with your anger.

1. This picture shows a short fuse. People who have a short fuse get angry very easily and may "explode" over things that seem little. People with a short fuse get upset about many things and feel very frustrated when things don't go their way. Their short fuse causes others to want to stay away from them.

2. This is a long fuse. People who have a long fuse tend to hold their feelings inside. They may feel very angry at another person but never talk to that person about what is causing their anger. People with long fuses tend to feel miserable inside and may even become sick because their feelings get stuck inside of them.

3. This is a balance. A balanced person feels anger and knows what to do with it. They neither hold their feelings inside or "blow up" at others. They talk to others about problems and conflicts as they happen and do things to feel better as described next.

Jamie Busby

C.O.P.

To find a balance in our lives, it is a good idea to have a **C.O.P.** A C.O.P. is short for Chill Out Plan. This is a plan where one chooses a few healthy things to do when anger arises. Below is a list of ideas kids have shared that have helped them to get over their anger. *Choose at least three or four things that you can do to chill out the next time you get angry.* The more you use your C.O.P., the better you'll get at handling anger. Your C.O.P. will become automatic after a while, so practice, practice, practice.

Ideas for Chill Out Plan

1. Talk to someone you trust
2. Conflict resolution (talk out the problem with the other person as soon as possible)
3. Count to ten or higher to calm down
4. Hit a pillow or punching bag
5. Positive self-talk (Use clear messages — see page 45.)
6. Walk away from an argument or teasing
7. Squeeze a ball
8. Read a book
9. Pray about it
10. Listen to music
11. Exercise
12. Get alone and scream
13. Take a time out
14. Take a deep breath
15. Write in a journal
16. Take a one-minute vacation (While *not* in class, imagine going to a favorite spot or doing a favorite activity.)
17. Break craft sticks
18. Enjoy a pet
19. Draw or paint your feelings
20. Write a letter (Even if you do not send it.)

My Chill Out Plan

List three to five ideas you can do to chill out when angry.

1. _____
2. _____
3. _____
4. _____
5. _____

5. Taking Control of My Life: Making Good Choices to Make My Life Better

A. Using Your Head and Heart

The first decision you need to make is that you *are* going to take care of yourself.

Perhaps your best two weapons are your head and heart. Your head, of course, involves using your brain power to make good decisions about how to act. Your heart is used to give you feelings about whether to do something or not. It is important to know how to listen to your feelings.

To use your *head*, always ask yourself these three questions before doing anything:

1. What am I getting ready to do?
2. What will happen if I do this?
3. What can I do instead?

Write these questions on a 3 x 5 inch index card or a small piece of paper. Carry it with you or tape it on your desk until you know them well. This card can be your "control card." Using your **heart** means listening or "tuning in" to your feelings. Your feelings are important and shouldn't be ignored. Try this: Write down the following promise used in the *Just Say No Club* on another card or sheet of paper.

Just Say No Promise #4

"I promise, if I ever have a scared, uncomfortable feeling inside about doing something, I'll just say no."

When you have the uh-oh feeling inside, your heart is telling you there is something wrong. Listen to your heart and think about doing the right thing.

Take the time to use your head and your heart. They are like two good friends. The split second it takes to think clearly and to notice your feelings will make the difference in getting along in school or not. It's up to you. You can control your behavior.

B. Listing Problem Areas or Life's Struggles

In order to take control of your life, you need to decide which of your personal worries are within or out of your control. The first step in doing this is to actually list the things that get you down. Think for a few minutes and write all of your worries on page 61.

1. _____
2. _____
3. _____
4. _____
5. _____
6. _____

C. Control Check

It is a good idea to divide your personal worries into two categories. (Those worries over which you feel you have control and those worries which you probably can't change no matter how hard you try.)

List your personal worries again, but this time write the worries that you feel you *can* control on the front burners of the stove top on page 62. Next list your personal worries that you feel you *can not* control on the back burners of the stove top.

Look below for an example of how this might be done.

This drawing can be helpful to you when you try to stay focused in a positive way at home and school.

Here is the example:

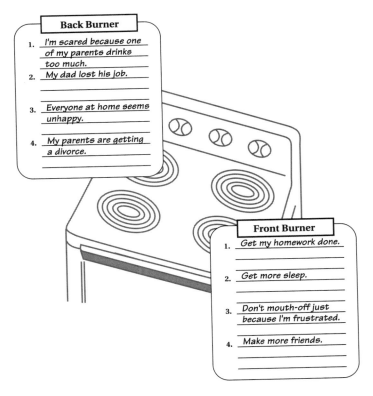

Back Burner
1. I'm scared because one of my parents drinks too much.
2. My dad lost his job.
3. Everyone at home seems unhappy.
4. My parents are getting a divorce.

Front Burner
1. Get my homework done.
2. Get more sleep.
3. Don't mouth-off just because I'm frustrated.
4. Make more friends.

Back Burner

1. _____
   _____
   _____

2. _____
   _____
   _____

3. _____
   _____
   _____

4. _____
   _____
   _____

Front Burner

1. _____
   _____
   _____

2. _____
   _____
   _____

3. _____
   _____
   _____

4. _____
   _____
   _____

Kim "Tip" Frank, Ed.S., LPC and Susan J. Smith-Rex, Ed.D.

The worries that you listed on the back burners don't mean that you don't care or don't want things to change. It just means that these worries are situations that at this time in your life will probably be there for a long time; and if they are taken off of the stove as a result of time or other circumstances, it probably wasn't a result of your actions.

The worries that you listed on the front burners are concerns that you can probably change with effort. These are concerns on which you *should* focus your energy.

Ask yourself the following questions:

1. What is it that you really want to change?

2. What are you doing now about the situation?

3. Are you willing to talk to people on your support team to make a plan that will help you get what you want?

4. Will you list at least three (3) specific things you can start to do to get or accomplish what you really want?

1. _____

2. _____

3. _____

4. _____

5. _____

These steps are good things to talk over with a trusted adult in your support team. While you have the ability to work out problems in your life, it is good to connect with an older person to review your plan.

Good Luck and Remember—**You can get over the blues**.

References

Frank, K.E., & Smith, S.J. (1993). *Children of alcoholics*. Rock Hill, SC: Winthrop University.

Frank, K.E., & Smith, S.J. (1994). *Getting a grip on ADD: A kid's guide to understanding and coping with attention disorders*. Minneapolis, MN: Educational Media Corporation.

Frank, K.E., & Smith-Rex, S.J. (1995). *Getting a life of your own: A kid's guide to understanding and coping with family alcoholism*. Minneapolis, MN: Educational Media Corporation.

Smith, S.J., & Walter, G. (1988). *Four steps to making friends*. Rock Hill, SC: Winthrop University.

Answers

All of the answers on page 39 are true.

Kim "Tip" Frank, Ed.S., LPC and Susan J. Smith-Rex, Ed.D.